Chinese New Year

Coloring Book For Kids

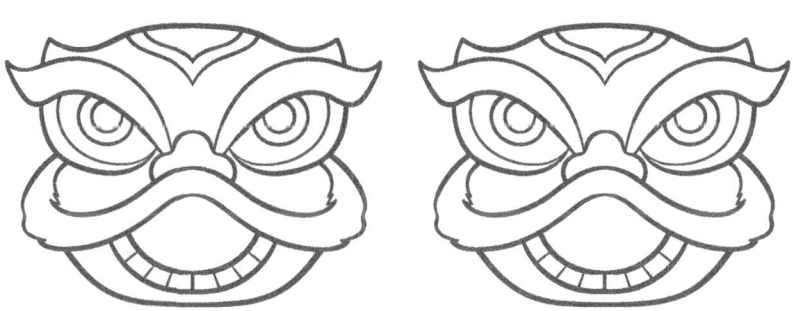

This Book Belongs to :

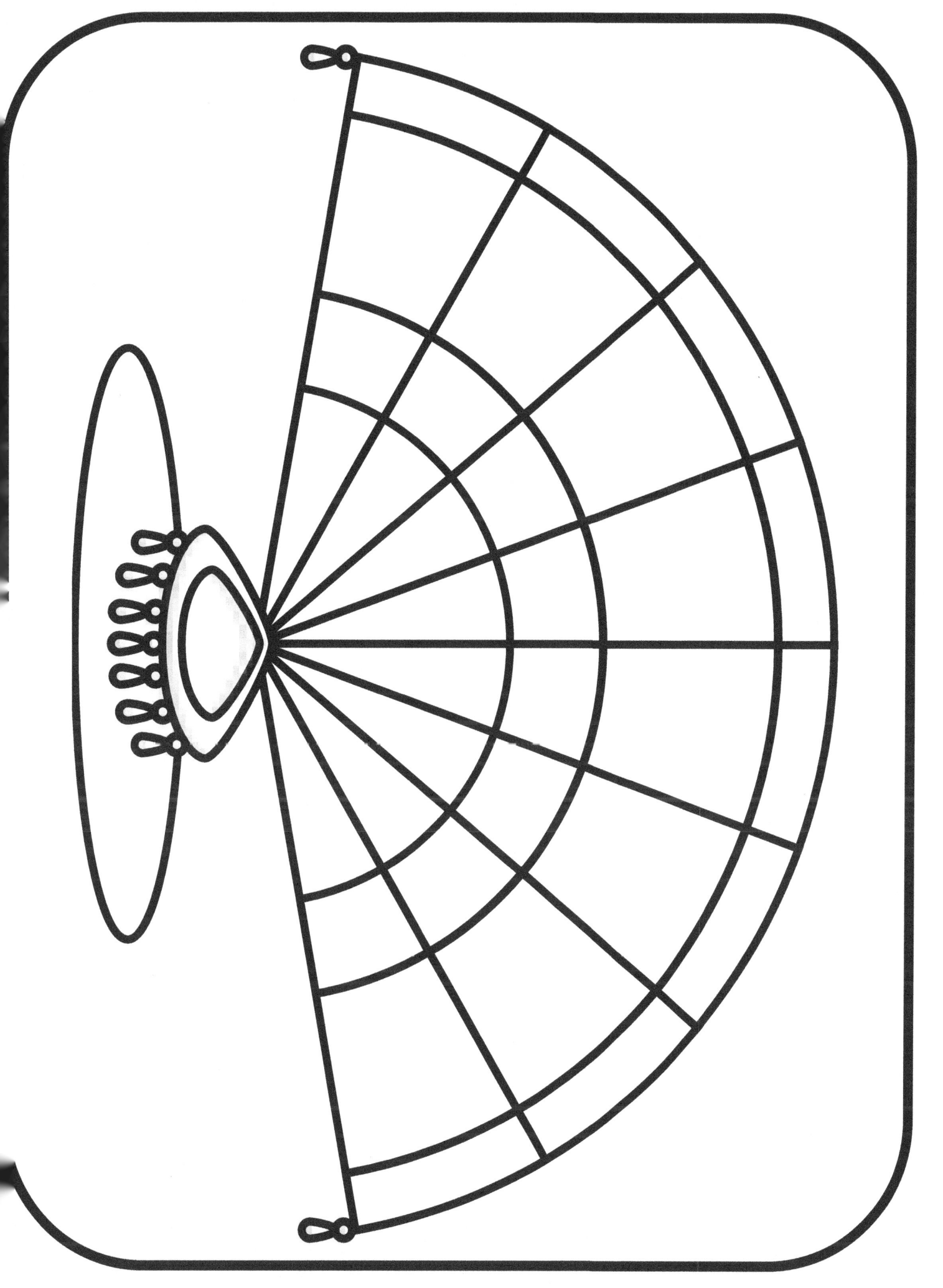

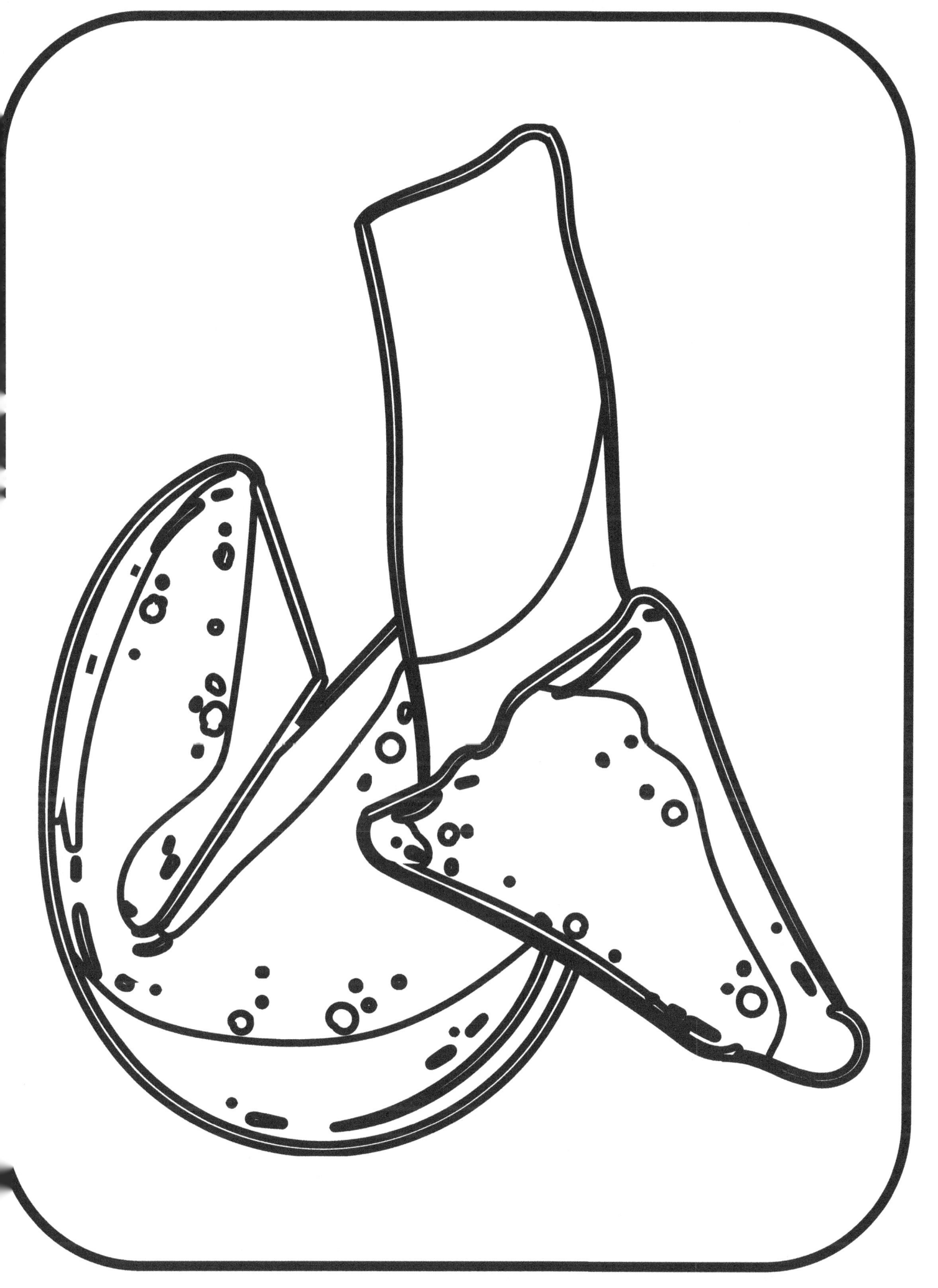

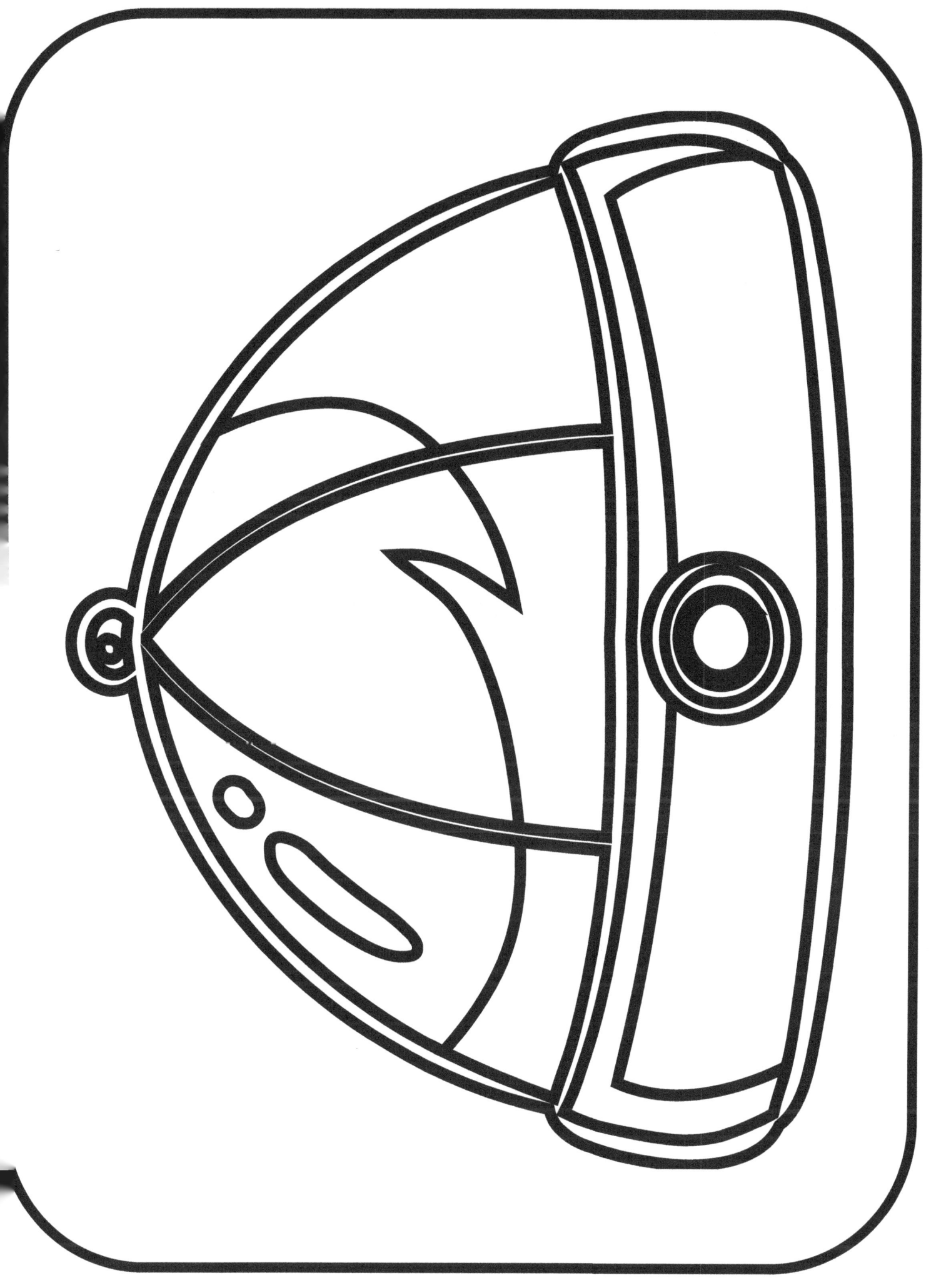

Wishing you prosperity

Chinese New Year

★★★★★

We Would like to Hear from You

Please leave a review on the website you purchased
this book so we can improve our product next time
And keep an eye out for more fun activity books
coming soon.

Made in United States
Orlando, FL
06 February 2024

43373314R00037